Samsung Galaxy S21 User Guide

A Simplified Manual For Beginners, Seniors And Pros, Used To Master Samsung Series, S21, S21 Plus And S21 Ultra With In-depth Details And Tips.

Whitney Volt

CONTENTS

CHAPTER ONE

Samsung s21 User Guide

Check the changes in the Galaxy S21 and S21+, the outlined camera design integrated in the device's metal case, updated matte and new colors like cool violet, gold-colored frame for a stylish effect.

The 6.2-inch screen S21 is a powerful AMOLED screen with a refresh rate of 120 Hz and provides smooth scrolling and viewing experience.

There's eye protection that automatically adjusts the level of blue light to reduce eye strain.

- The S21+ has the same AMOLED screen and eye protection, but the screen is larger 6.7 inches.
- S21 phone itself is the smallest in the series and measures 71.2 x 151.7 x 7.9 mm and the S21 + is 75.6 x 161.5 x 7.8 mm, so it is slightly larger.

Both phones have three cameras:

- This is a triple-camera camera with two pixels, a 12-megapixel main lens, a 12-megapixel extreme lens, and a 64-megapixel zoom lens. ,
- The camera captures an 8K video and can convert it to a high definition still image by clicking on the 8K video.
- One can see the scene at the same time, multiple angles and switch between lenses, new footage, to get a more accurate picture of the video you want.

The Vlogger section enable user can record with the front and rear cameras simultaneously to capture people's scenery and reactions. The phones also support the recording of many microphones to capture sound.

The Galaxy S21 Ultra possesses a four-pixel dual-pixel 12-megapixel extreme window and a 108 MP-megapixel wide-angle lens.

- There are two zoom lenses.
- The autofocus sensor, first introduced on the Note20 Ultra.
- This phone has 4K, 60 frames per second when all five lenses are taken,
- Including the front camera.
- The Galaxy S21 Ultra's screen is a 6.8-inch Edge WQHD + Dynamic AMOLED screen.
- Its refresh rate is 120 Hz.

The phone is the largest in the series and measures 75.6 x 165.1 x 8.9 mm. And it has the S Pen as an accessory for the first time in the Galaxy S series.

- The Ultra-Wide Band will be expanded to Ultra and S21 + devices.
- One can utilize the Galaxy S21 Ultra and Galaxy S21 + to open the car doors automatically without the key.
- Partnership with Google bring another integration in the car.
- Merging Android Auto experience with its software to allow a smooth car experience.

Before one get home, turn on the patio lights and even raise the room temperature when greeted on arrival.

What does it mean to use an S-pen on the Galaxy S21 Ultra?

There has been speculation that the S Pen's compatibility with the Galaxy S21 Ultra could mean that Samsung could end the future of the Note series.

Color options in the S21 series:

- In the US, the Galaxy S21 is available in Phantom Violet, Phantom Gray, Phantom Pink, and Phantom White models in 128GB and 256GB models with 8GB of RAM (256GB only available on Phantom Gray).
- Galaxy S21 + made in Phantom Violet, Phantom Silver, and Phantom Black formats in 128GB and

256GB models with 8GB of RAM (256GB only available on Phantom Black).

- Galaxy S21 Ultra is available in Phantom Black, Phantom Silver, Phantom Titanium, Phantom Navy, and Phantom Brown.

Phone pricing:

- Galaxy S21 starts at $799.99,
- Galaxy S21 + starts at $ 999.99
- Galaxy S21 Ultra starts at $ 1199.99.

Physical features of Galaxy S21

Screen:

- Displaying of 6.2 "flat FHD merged with AMOLED 2X Infinity-O screen (2400x1080)

Rear camera input:

- Triple, Ultra-wide: 12MP FF, FOV 120 ° F2.2, 1.4μm

Wide lens:

- 12MP Dual Pixel AF, OIS, F1.8, 1.8μm

Zoom lens:

- 64-megapixel phase detection focus, Hybrid Optic 3X, OIS F2.0, 0.8 μm
- 30x space travel

Front pixel:

- 10MP Dual Pixel AF, FOV 80 °, F2.2, 1.22μm

Battery:

- 4000 mAh

Dimensions:

- 71.2x151.7x7.9mm

Weight:

- 171g

Memory:

- 8GB RAM, 128GB/256GB internal storage

Network and connection:

- 5G Standalone (NSA), Standalone (SA), Sub6 / mmWave [Wi-Fi-6E] [Ultra-Wide Band]

Processor:

- Snapdragon 888, 5 nm 64-bit Octa-Core processor,
- It has 2.8 GHz, 2.4 GHz and 1.8 GHz
- Operating system: Android 11

Information about Galaxy S21 +

Screen:

- 6.7 "flat FHD + powerful AMOLED 2X Infinity-O screen (2400x1080)

Rear camera input:

- Triple, Ultra-wide: 12MP FF, FOV 120 ° F2.2, 1.4µm

Wide horn:

- 12MP Dual Pixel AF, OIS, F1.8, 1.8µm

Zoom lens:

- 64-megapixel phase detection focus, Hybrid Optic 3X, OIS F2.0, 0.8µm
- 30x space travel

Front pixel:

- 10MP Dual Pixel AF, FOV 80 °, F2.2, 1.22µm

Battery:

- 4800 mAh

Dimensions:

- 75.6x161.5x7.8mm

Weight:

- 202g

Memory:

- 8GB RAM, 128GB/256GB internal storage

Network and connection:

- 5G Standalone (NSA), Standalone (SA), Sub6 / mm Wave [Wi-Fi-6E] [Ultra-Wide Band]

Processor:

- Snapdragon 888, 5 nm 64-bit Octa-Core processor,
- 2.8 GHz (maximum clock speed) + 2.4 GHz + 1.8 GHz
- Operating system: Android 11

Information about Galaxy S21 Ultra

Screen:

- Displaying of 6.8 "Edge FHD merged with Dynamic AMOLED 2X Infinity-O screen (3200x1440)

Rear camera:

- Quad, very wide: 12MP Dual Pixel AF, FOV 120 °, F2.2, 1.4μm

Wide angle:

- 108MP phase detection focus, OIS, F1.8, 0.8μm

Zoom 1:

- 10MP Dual Pixel AF, 3x Optical, OIS, F2.4, 1.22μm

Zoom 2:

- 10MP Dual Pixel AF, 10x Optical, OIS, F4.9, 1.22μm
- 100x space drawing
- Laser focus sensor

Front camera:

- 40MP phase sensor AF, FOV 80 °, F2.2, 0.7 μm

Battery:

- 5000 mAh

Dimensions:

- 75.6x165.1x8.9mm

Weight:

- 229g

Memory:

- 12 GB RAM 128GB/256GB internal storage
- With 16GB RAM (LPDDR5) and 512GB ROM

Network and connection:

- 5G Standalone (NSA), Standalone (SA), Sub6 / mmWave [Wi-Fi-6E] [Ultra-Wide Band]

Processor:

- Snapdragon 888, 5 nm 64-bit Octa-Core processor,
- It has 2.8 GHz, 2.4 GHz and 1.8 GHz
- Operating system: Android 11

CHAPTER TWO

Starting With Samsung S21

The device uses a nano-SIM card.

- The SIM card may be pre-installed, or use previous SIM card.
- 5g network indicators are based on the settings and network availability of the network operator.

Install SIM/microSD card

- Insert the SIM card and optional microSD card into the tray with the gold-colored spot.

Fully charge the device battery.

- Use only Samsung- approved chargers and batteries.
- Samsung chargers and batteries are designed for your device to maximize battery life.
- The use of other chargers and batteries may void the warranty and cause damage.

The device is IP68 rated to withstand dust and water.

- To ensure waterproof and dustproof use of the device
- Make sure that there is no dust or water in the slots on the SIM card/memory cardholder
- The tray is inserted correctly before it enters liquid.

Battery

The device is powered by a rechargeable battery.

- The device has a charging head and USB Type-C cable to charge the battery from the wall socket.
- During use, the device, and the charger may become hot and stop charging.
- This does not normally affect the life or performance of the device and is within the normal range of the device.
- Disconnect the charger from the device and allow the device to cool down.

PowerShare Wireless

One can charge compatible Samsung devices wirelessly with phone.

- Under Quick Settings, tap Wireless PowerShare to activate this feature.
- Place the phone on a compatible device on the back of the phone to charge him down.
- Note that notification sound appears when charging starts.
- Wireless works with most Qi-certified devices.
- Requires at least 30% battery distribution.
- Download speed and efficiency vary by device.
- Incompatible with accessories, covers, or equipment from other manufacturers.
- If one has trouble connecting or the download is slow, remove the cover from each device.
- Poor call reception due to network

Get best results when using PowerShare Wireless:

- Eliminate extra accessories prior to usage.
- Based on the type of accessory.
- If not Wireless PowerShare performs poorly.
- The location of the wireless charging coil may vary from device to device.
- One may need to change the location to connect.
- The download starts, a vibration appears, so the notification shows connected.
- Depending on your network environment, this may affect the reception of calls or data services.
- Charging speed or efficiency may vary depending on the condition of the device or the environment.
- Do not use headphones.

Accessories

- One can configure accessories that are supported sold separately with settings.
- This option may not appear until you connect the accessory to device.
- Under Settings, tap Advanced> Accessories

Start using the device

- Turn on the device
- Activate the device with the side key.
- Don't use the appliance if the body is da

Please don't utilize the device till it has been restored.

- To enable switch on the device, press and hold the side key.
- To enable switch off device, open the Notification panel, and tap Power> Off.
- Confirm upon request.
- Enable restart device, open the Notification panel and click Power> Restart.
- Confirm upon request.
- One can also switch off the device by pressing the page and volume keys simultaneously.
- For more details on switching off the device, tap Advanced> Side key> Switch off the phone.

Use the setup wizard

- When you turn on your device for the first time, the setup wizard guides you through the basic steps of the device.
- Follow the instructions to select a Default language, connect to Wi-Fi® network, set up accounts, select location services, learn about device features, and more.

Transfer data from the old device

With Smart Switch you can transfer contacts, photos, music, videos, messages, notes, calendars, and more from your old device.

- Smart Switch can transfer data via USB cable, Wi-Fi, or PC.
- Under Settings, tap Accounts & backup> Smart switch.
- Follow the instructions and select the content you want to transfer.
- Hardware and software are constantly evolving - the images here are for reference only.
- Transporting material with a USB cable can increase the demand for battery power.
- Make sure the battery is fully charged.

Side key settings:

One can customize the shortcuts assigned to the page key.

- Double-click
- Select which feature is active when you press the side key twice.
- Under Settings, tap Advanced> Page key.

To enable this feature, double-tap, and tap:

- Quick Camera (default)
- Open Bixby
- Open the application
- Hold down
- Select which feature to start when you press and hold the side key.
- Under Settings, tap Advanced> Page key.
- Tap, Wake Bixby (default)
- Turn off the menu

User account

- Set up and manage your accounts.
- Invoices can support email, calendars, contacts, and other features.
- Contact operator for more detail.

Add a Google Account

Sign in to Google Account to access Google Cloud Storage account, apps installed by account, and get the most out of Android features.

- Under Settings, tap Accounts & backup> Accounts.
- Tap Add Account> Google.
- When you sign in to your Google Account, Factory Reset Protection (FRP) is activated.
- FRP requires that Google Account information be reset to factory settings.

Add a Samsung account

- Login Samsung account
- To access Samsung exclusive content
- Take full advantage of Samsung applications.
- Under Settings, tap Accounts & backup> Accounts.
- Tap Add Account> Samsung Account.
- Quickly access Samsung account
- Tap Samsung account profile under Settings.

Add an Outlook account

- Login to Outlook account to view and manage your email.
- Under Settings, tap Accounts & backup> Accounts.
- Tap Add Account> Outlook.

Setup answering machine

- One can set up a voicemail when you use it for the first time.
- One can use answering machine through the phone application.
- Press and hold 1 on the phone.
- Follow the instructions to create a password, save greeting, and save name.

Gestures

The touch screen responds best to the light touch of finger or the wider pen. Utilizing great pressure or metal items on the touch screen would harm the surface of the screen, noting the warranty doesn't cover it.

Tap
- Tap an item to select it.
- Press twice to zoom in or out.

Swipe
- Slightly drag your finger across the screen.
- Move gently on the screen to open the device.
- Move gently on the screen to navigate through the home screens/ menu options.

Drag and drop
- Hold the item and move it to a new location.
- Drag an app to add it to your home screen.
- Pull the device to relocate it.

Zoom in and out
- Zoom in and out by putting thumb and forefinger together or apart.
- Magnify by moving thumb and forefinger together on the screen.
- To zoom in, move thumb and forefinger apart on the screen.

Hold down
- Hold down objects to activate them.
- Hold down the box to display the popup menu options.
- Enable customize the home screen
- Press and hold the home screen.

Guide bar
- One can navigate device either with the navigation buttons or with gestures on the entire screen.

Navigation buttons
- Change the navigation icon screen at the bottom of the screen.
- In Settings, tap Display> Guideline.
- The following options are available:

Navigation buttons:
- Show the three navigation buttons at the bottom of the screen.

Button order
- Change the order of the back and recent applications icons.

Fullscreen gestures

- Hide navigation icons to use unobstructed display and use scrolling to scroll. The following options are available:

Advanced

- Configure advanced gesture settings in full screen.

Gesture tips:

- Show the lines at the bottom of the screen where each gesture is on screen.

Show keyboard hide button

- Show the icon in the lower right corner of the screen to hide the keyboard when the phone is in face mode.

All-in-one gesture options

- Further, customize gestures across the screen by adjusting the sensitivity and allowing different types of gestures.
- Settings>Display> Guideline> Full screen gestures> More options for

Swipe down

- Swipe up from three different areas at the bottom of the screen to go back, to the home screen, or to view the latest applications. One can also use the tool to swipe and hold the screen.

Swipe from the sides and bottom

- Swipe in from both sides of the screen to return, swipe from the bottom of the screen to go to the home screen, and move up and long press to view the latest apps.

Sensitivity to the gestures of the back

- Drag the slider to adjust the sensitivity of the device to notice gestures on the back.

CHAPTER THREE

Customize Home Screen

The better fact is that the home screen is the focal point for device navigation. Set favorite applications, also

- Set more home screens
- Delete screens,
- Rearrange the screen
- Select the main screen.

Application icon

- Launch the application from any home screen using the application icons.
- Hold down the application icon in applications and tap Add home.

To remove icons

- Via the Home screen, press and hold the application icon, then tap Remove from the home screen.
- Deleting an icon does not delete the application, it deletes the icon from the home screen.

Use folders

- Organize application shortcuts into folders in the Applications or Home screen.

Wallpaper

- To change the appearance of your home and lock screens, select your favorite photo, video, or pre-loaded wallpaper.
- From the Home screen, press and hold the screen, and then tap Wallpaper.

Tap one of the following menus to get wallpapers:

- My Wallpaper
- Select from the wallpaper currently displayed and download.

Gallery

- Select images and videos saved in Gallery.

Wallpaper service

- Enable advanced features, including instruction page and Quick-lock screen.

Use dark space for wallpaper

- Allow dark space to be applied to your wallpaper.

Explore other wallpapers:

- Find and download more wallpapers from Galaxy Themes.
- Tap a photo or video to select it.

If one selected an image

- Select the screen or screens for which one wants to use the wallpaper.

One can only use videos and multiple images for the lock screen.

- Tap Set on home screen
- Set on lock screen,
- Or set on home screen and lock the screen
- Depending on the screens you use.

If one set the wallpaper to both the home screen and the lock screen,

- Enable Sync My Changes
- If one wants the wallpaper to change on both screens.

Theme

Begin theme to use for home and lock screens, wallpapers, and application icons.

From the Home screen, press and hold.

- Tap Themes to customize.
- Tap a theme to preview it and upload it to My Themes.
- Hit My Page> Themes to enter downloaded themes.
- Tap a theme,
- Then tap Use to apply the selected theme.

Symbols

Use different symbols to replace the default symbols.

From the Home screen, press and hold.

- Tap Themes> Icons to customize.
- Tap an icon to preview it and paste it into my icons.
- Tap My Page> Icons to see the icons downloaded.
- Tap the icon,
- Then tap Use to use the selected character set.

Widgets

- Add gadgets to your home screen for quick access to data or applications.
- From the Home screen, press and hold.
- Tap and hold devices, drag and drop them to the home screen.

Create widgets

- Once you've added widgets, one can customize its location and behavior.

From the Home screen, hold down the device, then tap:

Remove from website:

- Remove the device from the screen.

Widget settings:

- Customize the function or appearance of the equipment.

Application Information:
- Check equipment usage, permissions, and more.

Home screen settings
- Edit the Home screen and the Applications screen.
- From the Home screen, press and hold.

Tap to customize the home screen settings:

- Home screen setup:
- Set up a separate home and application screen for your device, or just the home screen, where all your applications are located.

Home screen grid
- Select layout to determine how the icons are arranged on the home screen.
- Application network:
- Select layout to determine how the icons are arranged on the application screen.

Application Button
- Add a button to the Home screen for easy access to the Application screen.

Application icons

- Enables to display icons in applications with active notifications. You can also choose a font style.

Lock home screen layout

- Prevent items from being deleted or moved on the home screen.

Add applications to the Home screen:

- Automatically add recently downloaded applications to the Home screen.

Swipe down to get a notification card

- Allow this feature to swipe down on any home screen to open the notifications panel.

Rotate to landscape:

- Automatically rotate home screen when the device direction is changed from portrait to landscape.

Hide applications:

- Select an application to hide on the home screen and applications.
- Return to this screen to recover hidden applications.
- Hidden applications are installed and may appear as results in Finder searches.

About the Home screen

- View publishing information.

Easy mode

- Note that the Easy Mode mapping entails larger text and icons for great direct visual experience.
- One can switch between the default screen layout and a simpler display.

Application list

- In settings, tap Display> Easy mode.
- Tap to activate this feature. The following options appear:

Delay and Delay:

- Set how long it takes for continuous contact to be recognized as contact and hold.
- High Contrast Keyboard: Choose high-contrast color keyboards.

The status bar

- The status bar contains information about devices on the right and notification messages on the left.
- Status symbol

Notification icon

Set the display options for the status bar.
Under Quick settings, tap More options> Status bar to get the following settings:

Show notification icons:

- Select how notification icons appear in the status bar.

Show battery ratio:

- Show the battery ratio next to the battery icon on the status bar.

Notice panel

- Open notifications for quick access to notifications, settings, and more.

Show the bulletin board

One can access the Notification Card from any screen.

- Drag the status bar down to display the notification screen.
- Swipe down the list to see notification information.
- Tap an item to open it.
- Drag the notification left or right to clear one notification.
- Tap Clear to clear all notifications.
- Tap Notification settings to customize notifications.
- Swipe up from the bottom of the screen, or tap Back to close the notification panel.

Quick settings

The Notification Card also provides quick access to the device's features with quick settings.

- Drag the status bar down to display the notification screen.
- Drag Show All Down.
- Tap the speed dial icon to turn it on or off.
- Press and hold the quick-release icon to open the setting.
- Tap Find Search to search your device.
- Tap Power Off to turn off, restart, and emergency settings.

- Hit Open settings to enter the device settings menu.
- Tap more options to rearrange the speed settings or change the button bar.
- Drag Show All to close Quick Settings.

CHAPTER FOUR

Samsung Daily

Samsung Daily then displays custom content based on one's communication.

- Swipe to the right of the home screen.
- Add the Samsung Daily icon to the application list.
- Tap More options> Settings>
- Add Samsung Daily icon.

Customize Samsung Daily

In the More settings menu, you can add and organize maps, customize settings, and learn how to use Samsung Daily.

- Swipe to the right of the home screen.

Tap more options to get the following settings:

Cards:
- Tap a card to add it to your Samsung Daily site.

Settings:

- View the privacy policy, terms of use, and open-source licenses and add the Samsung Daily icon to the application list.

Announcements:

- Check out Samsung Daily Announcements.

Bixby

Bixby is a virtual assistant that learns, develops, and adapts to you.
- It learns your habits, helps you set reminders based on time and location, and is built into your favorite apps.
- Hold down the side key of the home screen.
- One can also use Bixby from the application list.

Bixby customs

- Bixby allows one to view information or change device settings based on your location and the situation you are creating.

- Under Settings, tap Advanced> Bixby Habits.

Bixby Visio

- Bixby is integrated with cameras, galleries, and Internet applications to give you a deeper idea of what you see.
- It provides contextual symbols for:
- Translations,
- QR code discovery,
- Landmark recognition, or commerce.

Camera
- Bixby Vision is available in the camera window so you can understand what you see.
- Tap More> Bixby Vision on the camera and follow the instructions.

Gallery
- Bixby Vision can be used for images stored in Gallery.
- Tap an image in Gallery to see it.
- Tap Bixby Vision and follow the instructions.

Internet
- Bixby Vision can help you get more information about the image found in the Internet application.
- Hold down an image on the Internet until a popup menu appears.
- Tap Bixby Vision and follow the instructions.

Digital wellness and child locking

One can monitor and control your digital habits by getting a daily view of how often you use applications, how many notifications you receive, and how often you check your device. One can also set the device to help you turn it off before going to bed. Tap Digital Welfare and Child Lock for Settings below

Showtime:

- Tap the time value on the overview screen to learn more about how long each app has been open and in use today.

Notifications:

- Tap to see how many notifications have been received for each application today.
- Open: Tap to see how many times each application has been open today.

Goals

- Set Showtime and open goals and look at daily averages.

Application timer

- Set a daily limit on the usage of each application.

Focus mode: Set time and actions to avoid interruptions in the phone.

Do not disturb:

- Turn on grayscale on screen and limit notifications before going to bed.

Volume control:

- Select a sound source to monitor the volume and protect your ears.

Child Lock:

- Track your child's digital life with Google Family Link.
- One can select applications, set content filters, monitor screen time, and set screen time limits.

Always on screen

View missed calls and message notifications, check the time and date and view other custom information without opening the device in (Always on-screen) mode.

- Via settings, tap Lock screen> Always-on screen.
- Tap to activate the function, and then set the following settings:
- Select when to watch and a message appears on the screen when the device is not used
- Tap to show, Show always show or schedule.

Clock style:
- Change the clock style and color options on the lock screen and always on the screen.

Show music information:
- Use Face Widgets Music Manager
- Rotate the screen to Display AOD in face or landscape mode.

Auto brightness:
- Set brightness automatically to Always-on screen.

About Always On Display:
- View current software release and
- View license information.
- Some display settings can be displayed on both the lock screen.
- Always on the screen.

AOD theme

- Use custom Always On Display themes.
- From the Home screen, press, and then tap Themes> AOD.
- Tap AOD to preview
- Upload to Always On Display.
- Tap My Page> AODs to see downloaded AODs.
- Tap AOD, then tap Apply.

Biological statistical security
- Open your device and log in to your accounts with biometrics.

Face recognition
- One can enable face recognition to open the screen.
- To open the device with face,
- One need to set a pattern, PIN, or password.
- Face detection is more insecure than a pattern, PIN, or password.
- One device may have been accessed by someone or someone similar to photo.
- Some conditions can affect facial recognition,
- Including the use of glasses, hats, beards, or heavy make-up.
- When recording face, make sure one is in a well-lit area and that the camera lens is clean.

Under Settings, tap Biometrics & Security> Face Detection.

- Follow the instructions to register your face.
- Face recognition management
- Customize facial recognition behavior.
- Under Settings,
- Tap Biometrics & Security> Face Detection.

Delete facial data
- Delete existing faces.

Add a different look
- Improve facial recognition by adding a different look.

Face detection:
- Enable or disable face detection protection.

Remain on the lock screen:
- When one gain entrance into the device with Face Detection,
- Be on the lock screen till one gently swipe the screen.

Faster detection:
- Enable faster face detection.
- Turn it off to increase security and make it harder to access a photo or video of choice.

Require open eyes:
- Face Detection only recognizes face when your eyes are open.

Clear screen
- Temporarily up the screen brightness to recognize face in the dark.

CHAPTER FIVE

Samsung Pass

- Open online accounts with face recognition.
- Use fingerprint to authenticate when using support applications.

Biometric Lock:
- Learn more about protecting device with biometrics.

Fingerprint sensor

- Use fingerprint authentication as an option when entering passwords in specific applications.
- One can also use fingerprint to verify the signee via Samsung account.
- To access the device with fingerprint, enter a pattern, PIN, or password.
- Under Settings,
- Tap Biometrics & Security> Fingerprints.

Follow the instructions to register your fingerprint.

- Fingerprint control
- Add, delete and rename fingerprints.

Under Settings, tap Biometrics & Security> Fingerprints to get the following settings:

- The list of registered fingerprints is at the top of the list.
- Tap the fingerprint to delete or rename it.

Add a fingerprint:

- Follow instructions to register another fingerprint.

Check fingerprints:
- Check fingerprint to see if it is listed.

Fingerprint confirmation settings
- Use fingerprint authentication to verify in supported applications and features.
- Under Settings,
- Tap Biometrics & Security> Fingerprints.

To open the fingerprint
- Use the fingerprint to authenticate when you open the device.

Show icons when the screen is off:
- Show fingerprints when the screen is off.

Samsung Pay:
- Make payments with your fingerprints quickly and securely.

For biological number locks

Read the requirements for each biological security feature to use a pattern, PIN, or password as a backup.

Biological statistical settings

- Configure biostatistics security options.
- Under Settings,
- Tap Biometrics and Security> Biometrics to:
- Screen Transform Effect:
- Show transition effects when using biometric data to unlock the device.
- Under Settings,
- Tap Biometrics and Security> Biometrics Security patch
- To see the software version of the device's biological security features.

Mobile continuity

Calls, messages, video and video storage, and other features of device can be used and integrated with compatible mobile phones and computers.

Link to Windows

Achieve mobile continuity between Samsung device and Windows PCs. Connect device with quick access to pictures, messages, and other devices on device.

Pictures

- Drag and drop images into Windows.
- Open and edit pictures in My pictures.
- Share photos with your contacts through Windows.

Messaging (SMS / MMS)

- Communication support with MMS group.
- Integration with Windows Emoji Picker.
- Get Windows pop-up when you receive a new message.

Notifications

- Manage phone announcements via computer
- Exclude notifications for each applications.
- Get a Windows pop-up when one receives a new notification.

To mirror the program

- Stream your phone screen to your computer.
- Communicate with your phone with the keyboard and mouse.
- Use Windows access.

Connect device to computer

- Under Settings, tap Advanced> Link to Windows.
- Tap to activate this feature.
- Follow the instructions to connect your device to computer.
- One can also enable this feature in the Quick Settings menu.

Samsung DeX for PC
- Connect device to computer for better multitasking.
- Use device and computer applications at the same time.
- One can share the keyboard, mouse, and screen via two devices.
- Call or send SMS when using DeX.

Set up DeX on computer
- Connect mobile phone to your computer with a standard USB-C cable.
- Follow the instructions on device when downloading and installing DeX for PC software on computer.

Call and send a text to other devices

This feature allows one to make and receive calls and text messages from Galaxy device that are logged into Samsung account.

- Under Settings, tap Advanced> Calls and text on other devices.
- Tap to activate the function.
- The connection is made automatically.
- Log in to Samsung account on Galaxy devices.
- Transfer contacts from phone to Samsung account so that one can access them on all registered devices.

Multi-window

- The use of multiple applications simultaneously.
- Programs that support multiple windows can be displayed on a single swap screen.
- One can switch between applications and adjust the size of their windows.
- Tap Recent applications from any screen.
- Tap the application icon, then tap Open in two types of screen.
- Tap an application in another window to add it to the switch screen.
- Drag the center of the window to adjust the size of the window.

Edge screen

The Edge screen consists of several customizable edging boards. Edge panels are utilized for applications, tasks, and contacts, likewise viewing news, sports and others.

Application panel

- One can add up to ten applications in two columns on the application screen.
- Drag the Edge handle on any screen to the center of the screen.
- Swipe until the application card appears.
- Tap an application or application pair to open it.
- To configure the application card:
- Drag the Edge handle on any screen to the center of the screen. Swipe until the application card appears.
- Tap Add apps in folder to add other apps to the apps screen.
- To add an app to the Apps panel, find it on the left side of the screen and tap it to add the right column to the available space.
- To create a shortcut for two applications to open in multiple windows, tap Create application pair.
- To create a folder shortcut, drag an application from the left side of the screen to the application in the right-hand columns.
- To change the order of applications in the panel, drag each application to its desired location.
- Tap Remove to uninstall the application.
- Tap Back to save changes.

Smart selection

The smart selection feature saves an image or video as an image area that you can share or attach to the screen.

- Drag the Edge handle on any screen to the center of the screen. Swipe until the Smart select panel appears.
- Tap the smart dial you want to use:

Rectangle

- Captures the rectangular area of the screen.

Oval

- Covers the oval area of the screen.

Video

- Save the function on the screen as a video GIF file.

Attach to screen

- Capture the area and attach it to the screen.

Tools

- The Tools panel provides convenient tools for quick access.
- Drag the Edge handle on any screen to the center of the screen. Swipe until the Tools panel appears.
- Tap the tool you want to use:

Compass:

- Familiar with compass.
- Tap Calibrate to calibrate the compass.

Numerator:

- Add or subtract plus and minus symbols when counting.
- Tap Vibrate To turn the vibration on or off with each increase or decrease.
- Tap Destination to set the total number of limits between 1 and 9999.
- Tap Reset to reset the counter.

Flashlight:

- Hit Flashlight to turn on and off.
- Use plus and minus symbols to increase or decrease the brightness of the light.
- Tap SOS for the flashlight to mark the phrase "SOS" in the Morse code.

Surface level

- One can use the device to determine if the surface is flat by placing it on the surface.
- The surface is smooth when the x and y values are close to zero degrees or equal.
- Tap Calibrate to adjust the level.

Control

- Use the edge of the device like a ruler to measure a straight line in inches or centimeters.
- Tap the unit name to edit units.

Adjust Edge panels

- One can customize Edge panels.
- Tap Settings on the Edge screen.
- Tap to activate the function.

The following options are available

- Check box: Enable or disable each panel.
- Edit (if available): Define individual panels.
- Search: Search for installed or installed panels.

More options

- Rearrange Drag left or right to rearrange panels.
- Remove: Remove the Edge panel from your device.
- Handle settings: Change the position and style of the Edge handle.

Galaxy Store

- Find and download more Edge cards from Galaxy Store.
- Tap Back to save changes.

Location of the board

- One can modify the position of the Edge handle.
- Tap Settings on the Edge screen.
- Tap More options>
- Processing settings for the following options:

Edge Handle

- Drag to return the edge handle to the edge of the screen.

Position

- Select either right or left to set which side of the Edge screen appears.

Handle position lock

- Activates to prevent the handle position from moving when touched and held.

Edge panel style
- Change the style of the Edge handle.
- Tap Settings on the Edge screen.
- Tap More options>
- Processing settings for the following options:

Colors
- Select the color of the Edge handle.

Transparency
- Move the slider to modify the transparency of the Edge handle.

Size
- Move slider to change the size of the Edge handle.

Special notification

Adjust the Edge screen to appear when one receives calls or notifications, and make alerts visible even with the screen facing down.

- In Settings,
- Tap Display> Edge display> Edge description.
- Tap to activate the function.

Light style
- Change the color, width, and transparency of the browning function.
- In Settings,
- Tap Display> Edge display> Edge description.

Tap Light Style to customize

- Impact: Select the edge effect.

Color

- Select a preset or custom color and activate the application color.
- Tap Add Keywords to set a custom light effect for a specific text that appears in ad titles.

Advanced

- Set other Edge lighting features.

Transparency

- Drag the slider to adjust the transparency of the Edge description.

Width

- Move the slider to change the width of the border.

Length

- Drag the slider to set how short or long the Edge light appears.
- When done, tap done.

Show Edge description

- Choose when Edge lighting replaces notifications.
- In Settings,
- Tap Display> Edge display> Edge description.
- Tap Show border description to select

When the screen is on:

- Edge lighting replaces notification pop-ups.

When the screen is off:

- The edge light replaces the message that turns on the screen.

Always:

- Show the edge light for all notifications, regardless of whether the screen is on or off.

About the Edge screen

- One can view the current software release and license information for the Edge screen saver.
- In Settings, tap Display> Edge display> Edge info screen.

CHAPTER SIX

Set Up Samsung Keyboard

Tap Settings on the Samsung keyboard to get the following settings:

Languages and Types:

- Set the keyboard type and use the keyboard to select the available languages.
- Swipe left or right to switch between languages.

Smart typing:

- Use predictive text and auto-correction features to avoid common typos.
- Swipe between letters to enter.

Style and look:

- Customize the look and feel of keyboard.

Swipe, touch and respond:

- Customize gestures and feedback.

Restore default settings:

- Restore keyboard to its original settings and delete personal information.

Set Samsung audio input

- Set custom options for Samsung audio input.
- Tap the audio input on the Samsung keyboard.
- Tap Settings to see the options.

Keyboard language:
- Select the keyboard language.

Input language:
- Select the language of the audio input language.

Hide offensive words:
- Hide potentially offensive words with constellations.

About Samsung Audio Input:

- View the release and legal information of Samsung Audio Input.

Emergency

Use emergency mode to use useful emergency features and save energy in an emergency.

To save battery in an emergency:

- Restricts the use of applications only to applications that are necessary and selected.
- Turns off connection features and mobile data when the screen is turned off.

Activate emergency mode

- Open the notification panel and tap Power.
- Tap Emergency Number.
- When using for the first time, read and accept the terms of use.
- Tap Activate.

Emergency measures

In emergency, only the following applications and functions are available on the home screen:

Flashlight

- Use the device flash as a steady light source.
- Emergency alert: ring the siren.

Camera and Gallery

- One can take high-quality photos and videos with the Camera application.
- Images and videos are saved in Gallery, where you can view and edit them.

Camera

Enjoy all kinds of professional lenses and video formats and settings in professional quality.

- In Applications, tap Camera.
- If Quick Launch is enabled, quickly press the side button twice.

Navigate the camera screen

- Take great pictures with the front and rear cameras.
- Adjust the camera from the camera with the following features:
- Tap the screen you want the camera to focus on.
- When you tap the screen, the brightness scale is displayed. Drag the circle to adjust the brightness.
- Quickly switch between front and rear cameras by swiping the screen up or down.
- To switch to another photoshoot, swipe left or right.
- Tap Settings to change the camera settings.
- Tap Capture.

Adjust the shooting mode

- The camera determines the preferred mode for your pictures, or select from several shooting modes.
- To change the shooting mode, swipe the screen left and right across the camera.

Photo:

- Let the camera determine the preferences for your photos.

Video:

- Set the camera to set video preferences.

Simple shot:

- Tap the shutter-release button to take a series of shots and short videos of the scene.
- Add Select other available shooting methods.
- Tap Edit to drag settings into or out of the Mode tray at the bottom of the camera screen.

Pro:

- Details of manual ISO sensitivity, exposure value, white balance, and color tones when taking pictures.

Panorama:

- Create a linear image by taking pictures either horizontally or vertically.

Food:

- Take pictures that emphasize the bright colors of the food.

Night:

- Use this to take pictures in low light without the flash.

Live focus:

- Capture artistic images by adjusting the depth of field.

Take a screenshot

- Take picture of screen.
- The device automatically creates a Screenshot album in Gallery.
- Press the page and volume buttons of any screen.
- Swipe with your palm to take the screenshot
- To take a picture of the screen,
- Swipe the edge of hand over it and hold it from side to side.
- In settings, tap Details>
- Gestures and gestures> Swipe to capture.
- Tap to activate this feature.

Screenshot settings
- Control screen and recording settings.
- Under Settings,
- Tap Advanced> Screenshots and screenshots.

Screenshot toolbar
- Show advanced settings after taking a screenshot.

Delete shared screenshots:
- Automatically delete screenshots when shared via the screenshot bar.

Screenshot format
- Select screenshots to be saved as JPG or PNG files.

Screen recorder

Record activities on device, record notes, and use the camera to record a video manager for one to share with friends or family.

- To start recording, tap the Screen recorder in quick settings.
- Tap Draw to draw on the screen.
- Tap Selfie video to add recording from the front of your camera.
- Tap Stop to stop recording.
- These are saved automatically on the recording folder in the Gallery screen.

Display recording settings
- Controls the audio and quality settings of the screen recording.
- Under Settings,
- Tap Advanced>
- Then Screenshots/recording >
- Lastly tap settings.

Sound

- Select the sounds to be recorded when using the screen recorder.

Video quality

- Select the resolution. Choosing a higher resolution to increase quality requires more memory.

Selfie video size

- Drag the slider to resize the video.

Arrange applications

- Application shortcuts can be listed in alphabetical order or custom order.
- Under Applications, tap More options>
- Sort to get the following sorting options:

Custom order:

- Arrange applications manually.

Alphabetical order:

- Arrange programs in alphabetical order.

Once the applications have been manually sorted, remove the empty icon space, clicking More Options> Clear Pages.

Create and use folders

- Create folders to organize shortcuts to applications in the application list.
- Tap and hold an app in the app, and then drag it over another application shortcut until it is highlighted.
- Release the applet to create a folder.
- Folder name: Give the folder a name.
- Palette: Change the color of the folder.

Add applications:
- Add more applications to the folder.
- Tap applications to select them, then tap done.
- Tap Back to close the folder.

Copy the folder to the Home screen
- One can copy a folder to the home screen.
- In applications, hold down a folder
- Tap Add home.

Delete the folder
Delete a folder, the applications return to the application list shortcuts.

- In applications, press and hold the folder you want to delete.
- Tap Delete folder and confirm when prompted.

Game booster

- Get optimized by playing games based on usage.
- Block calls or other notifications and enable features like Bixby or Dolby Atmos.
- While playing the game, swipe up from the bottom of the screen to see the navigation bar.

The following options appear on the right and left:

Touch screen lock:

- Lock the screen to prevent accidental knocking. This is the default setting.

Game Booster:

- More options, performance monitoring, and close the navigation bar, touch screen, and screenshots.

CHAPTER SEVEN

Application Settings

- Manage pre-downloaded/pre-installed applications.
- The options vary by application.
- In Settings, tap Applications.
- Tap More options to get the following settings:

Sort by
- Sort applications by size, name, last used, or last updated.

Default applications:
- Select or change the applications that are default for certain features, such as email or web browsing.

Access control
- Control which applications have access to certain features of device.

Show/hide system application
- Show or hide system application (background).

Special access
- Select which applications can have special access to the device features.

Reset application settings
- Reset changed settings.
- Existing application data will not be deleted.
- Tap an application to view and update application information.
- The following options may appear:

Usage Mobile data:

- View mobile data usage.

Battery:

- View battery usage from the last charge.

Storage:

- Manage the storage usage of the application.

Memory:

- View memory usage. Application settings

Notifications:

- Set notifications for the application.

Sources:

- Check the application permissions for the equipment data.

Set as default:

- Set application as default for a specific application category. Advanced
- The options vary by application. Application information options

Open:

- Launch the application.
- Not all applications have this feature.

Disable / Disable:

- Disable or disable the application.
- Some preloaded programs may be disabled,
- Or not removed.

Force shutdown:

- Stop a program that is not working properly.

Galaxy portable

- Connect device to Samsung Watch with this application.
- Tap Galaxy Wearable in applications.

Game launcher

- Automatically organize all your games in one place
- Tap Game Launcher in Applications.
- If Game Launcher does not appear in the Apps list, then tap About
- Advanced> Game launcher, then tap.

Samsung's Global goals

- Read more about the initiative on world goals and present contributions,
- Support these reasons with ads in this application.
- In apps, tap Samsung's World Goals.

Samsung members

- Get more and more out of your Galaxy device.
- Enjoy DIY support tools and exclusive rights

Experience and content

- Only for Samsung members. Samsung members can be preload on device
- Or you can download and install it from the Galaxy Store or

Google Play Store.

- Under Applications, tap Samsung folder> Samsung members.

Mapping problems

- One can check for software updates and, if necessary, reset the service on your device.

Software update

- Check for and install software updates for device.
- Under Settings,
- Tap Software Update to get the following settings:

Download and install:

- Check software updates are installed and if available.

Latest update:

- View information of current software installation.

Reset

- Reset device and network settings.
- One can also reset your device to factory settings.

Reset settings

- One can reset device to factory settings,
- Which reset everything except security, language, and account settings.
- Personal information does not affect.
- Under Settings,
- Tap General management> Reset> Reset settings.
- Tap Reset settings and confirm when prompted.

Reset network settings

- Select Reset network settings to reset Wi-Fi, mobile data, and Bluetooth settings.
- Under Settings,
- Tap General management>
- Reset> Reset network settings.
- Tap Reset settings and confirm when prompted.

Before resetting the device

- Make sure the data you want to store has been moved to your storage area.
- Log in to Google Account and verify your username and password.
- To reset device:
- In Settings,
- Tap General management> Restore> Restore factory settings.
- Tap Reset and follow the instructions to reset.
- When restarting the device, follow the instructions for setting up the device.

Factory reset

- When one signs in to device's Google Account, the factory reset protection (FRP) is activated.
- FRP prevents others from using the device if it is reset to factory settings without your permission.
- If device is lost or stolen and factory reset is needed, only someone with Google Account username and password can use the device.

One will not be able to use the device after factory data reset if no Google Account username and password.

Before sending device to Samsung or transferring it to an authorized Samsung service center, delete Google Account and restore the factory settings.

Enable factory default protection

- Adding a Google Account to your device enables the FRP security feature.

Disable factory default protection

- Turn off FRP by deleting all Google Accounts from your device.
- Under Settings,
- Tap Accounts & Backups>
- Accounts> [Google Account].
- Tap Delete account.

Collect analyzes

- Collect diagnostic information for problems.
- In Settings,
- Tap General management>
- Reset> Collect diagnostics.

The following options are available:

Diagnosis:
- Help T-Mobile troubleshoot with device.

Troubleshooting:
- Optimize Wi-Fi connections and diagnose network problems.

Personal Offers:
- Get T-Mobile Offers That Improve You experience.

Set a secure screen lock

It is recommended to protect your device with a secure screen lock (pattern, PIN, or password). This is necessary for the installation and promotion of biological locks.

In Settings, tap Lock screen> Screen lock type, then tap a secure screen lock (pattern, PIN, or password).

- Tap to display notifications on the lock screen.

The following options are available:

Show style:
- Show or hide notification information and show only the icon.

Hide content:
- Do not show notifications in the notifications panel.

Notifications to display:
- Select the notifications that appear on the lock screen.

Always show on screen:
- Always show notifications on screen.
- When done, tap Done.

Set the following screen lock settings:

Smart Lock
- Directly unlock the device when trusted locations or other devices are found.
- A fortified screen lock is required for this feature.

Secure lock settings
- Customize the security lock settings.

Always on screen:

- Always turn on the screen.

Google Play Protect
- One can install Google Play to regularly scan application and device for security risks and threats.
- Under Settings,
- Tap Biometrics and Security> Google Play Protect.
- Updates are marked automatically.

Find my cell phone

- One can protect device from damage or theft by locking it, monitoring it online, and deleting data remotely.
- One needs a Samsung account and Google's location must be turned on to use Find My Mobile.

Activate Find my mobile phone

- Before you can use Find My Mobile, you need to turn it on and customize your options.
- If one wanted to use device remotely,
- Go to findmymobile.samsung.com.
- Under Settings,
- Tap Biometrics & Security>
- Find mobile phone.
- Tap To turn on Find My Mobile and sign in to your Samsung account.

The following options are available:

Remote lock

- Allow Samsung to save your PIN, pattern, or password to open and remotely control your device.

Share last location

- Enable device to deliver its last location to Find My Mobile server when the leftover battery has a minimal percentage.

CHAPTER EIGHT

Security Update

One can easily check the date of the last installed security software update and see if newer updates are available.

- Under Settings,
- Tap Biometrics & Security>

Security Update to see the latest security update installed and check for a new update.

Samsung Pass

Utilize Samsung Pass to gain entrance into favorite services via biometrics.

- Login Samsung account to use a Samsung passport.
- Under Settings,
- Tap Biometrics and Security> Samsung Pass.
- Login Samsung account
- Add biological information.

Samsung Blockchain keyboard

Manage the private key of the blockchain.

- Under Settings,
- Tap Biometrics & Security>
- Samsung Blockchain Keystore.
- Follow the instructions to import or configure a new wallet.

Install unknown program

One can allow selected applications or sources of unknown third-party application

- Under Settings,
- Tap Biometrics & Security>
- Install Unknown Application.
- Tap an application or source, then tap Allow from this source.

Installing unknown third-party applications may make your device and personal data more vulnerable to security risks.

Adjust the SIM card lock

One can set a PIN code to lock SIM card, which will prevent unauthorized use of the SIM card if someone else tries to use it.

- Under Settings,
- Tap Biometrics & Security>
- Other security settings> Set up SIM card lock and follow the instructions.
- Tap Lock SIM card to activate the function.
- To change a new PIN,
- Tap Change SIM PIN.

Show password

Make characters appear instantly in the password fields when enter them.

- Under Settings,
- Tap Biometrics & Security>
- Other security settings>
- Make password visible to activate the feature.

Device management

One can authorize security features and applications such as Find My Mobile Phone to use administrator privileges on device.

- Under Settings,
- Tap Biometrics & Security>
- Other security settings> Device application.
- Tap an option to turn it on as the device controller.

Label storage

One can manage trusted security certificates installed on device, which verifies the authentication of servers for a secure connection.

- Under Settings,
- Tap Biometrics & Security>

Other security settings for the following settings:

Save type:

- Select where the credentials are stored.

View security certificates:

- View the certificates on your device's ROM and any other certificates you have installed.

User certificates:

- Detail user certificates that signify device.

Install via device storage:

- Save a new certificate via storage.

Clear credentials:

- Delete credentials from your device and reset your password.

Advanced security settings

These settings allow to configure advanced settings to better protect device.

- Under Settings,
- Tap Biometrics & Security>
- Other security settings for the following settings

Trusted Agents:

- Allow trusted devices to perform the selected operation while connected.
- This option appears only when the lock screen is on. For more information.
- Set up a secure screen lock.

Fix window:

- Fix the application on the device screen to prevent access to other device features.

Security policy updates:

- Check for security updates to keep device safe.

Account

One can link and manage accounts, including

- Google Account
- Samsung account
- Email address
- Social networking account.

Samsung cloud

- One can keep data safe by backing up and restoring your device.
- Synchronize data from multiple devices.
- Under Settings,
- Tap Accounts & backup>
- Samsung Cloud.
- If no Samsung account has been added, the screens will tell how to create or sign in to account.
- Once a Samsung account has been set up, you can view and manage the items stored in the Samsung cloud.

Add an account

- One can add and sync all your email, social networking, and share accounts with photos and videos.
- Under Settings,
- Tap Accounts & backup>
- Accounts> Add account.
- Tap one of the account types.
- Enter your username and
- Follow the instructions to set up account.
- Tap Automatic data synchronization
- To turn on automatic updates for your account.

Account settings

Each account has its custom settings. Set common settings for all accounts of the same type.

- Account settings
- Available features vary by account type.
- Under Settings, tap Accounts & backup> Accounts.
- Enter account to start the sync settings.
- Tap other options available for account creation.

Remove account

- One can delete accounts from your device.
- Under Settings, tap Accounts & backup> Accounts.
- Tap the account, then tap Delete Account.

Backup and recovery

- One can set up device to back up data to Samsung account
- One can back up data to Samsung account.
- Under Settings,
- Tap Accounts & backup>

Backup and restore for options:

- Back up data
- Set up Samsung account to back up data.

Recover data:

- Recover the backup data to Samsung account.

Google Account

- One can copy data to Google Account.
- Under Settings,
- Tap Accounts & backup>
- Backup and restore for options:

Back up data:

- Engage in backup of apps data, Wi-Fi passwords, and various settings relying on Google's servers.
- Duplicate account: Select the Google Account that will be used as the duplicate account.

Automatic recovery:

- One can enable automatic settings recovery through Google servers.